YOUR KNOWLEDGE HAS VALUE

- We will publish your bachelor's and master's thesis, essays and papers

- Your own eBook and book - sold worldwide in all relevant shops

- Earn money with each sale

Upload your text at www.GRIN.com
and publish for free

Bibliographic information published by the German National Library:

The German National Library lists this publication in the National Bibliography; detailed bibliographic data are available on the Internet at http://dnb.dnb.de .

This book is copyright material and must not be copied, reproduced, transferred, distributed, leased, licensed or publicly performed or used in any way except as specifically permitted in writing by the publishers, as allowed under the terms and conditions under which it was purchased or as strictly permitted by applicable copyright law. Any unauthorized distribution or use of this text may be a direct infringement of the author s and publisher s rights and those responsible may be liable in law accordingly.

Imprint:

Copyright © 2017 GRIN Verlag, Open Publishing GmbH
Print and binding: Books on Demand GmbH, Norderstedt Germany
ISBN: 9783668549692

This book at GRIN:

http://www.grin.com/en/e-book/376903/biclustering-algorithms-for-microarray-data

Rengeswaran Balamurugan

Biclustering Algorithms for Microarray Data

GRIN Publishing

GRIN - Your knowledge has value

Since its foundation in 1998, GRIN has specialized in publishing academic texts by students, college teachers and other academics as e-book and printed book. The website www.grin.com is an ideal platform for presenting term papers, final papers, scientific essays, dissertations and specialist books.

Visit us on the internet:

http://www.grin.com/

http://www.facebook.com/grincom

http://www.twitter.com/grin_com

Biclustering Algorithms for Microarray Data

R. Balamurugan

Associate Professor, Department of Computer Science and Engineering, Bharat Institute of Engineering and Technology, Hyderabad, India

Abstract

DNA microarray aims at extracting useful information that can be applied in medical and biological studies. Clustering is one of the most utilized data mining technique to analyze the gene expression data. Generaly, there are subsets of genes that have similar behave or under subsets of conditions. Therefore, biclustering term is introduced to identify the subgroups of genes and subgroups of conditions by performing simultaneous clustering of both rows and columns of the gene expression matrix, rather than clustering these two dimensions separately. In this comprehensive survey, we tend to analyze a large number of existing methods to biclustering, and classify them in accordance with the methods used to perform the search.

Keywords: Biclustering, microarray, genes, optimization, expression data.

1. INTRODUCTION

DNA microarray technologies have made it feasible to monitor transcription levels of tens of thousands of genes in a single expriment. A typical DNA microarray experiment involves a multistep procedure: fabrication of microarrays by fixing properly designed oligonucleotides representing specific genes; hybridization of cDNA populations onto the microarray; scanning hybridization signals and image analysis; transformation and normalization of data; and analyzing data to identify differentially expressed genes as well as sets of genes that are co regulated [1]. A gene expression data set from a microarray experiment can be represented by a real-valued expression matrix. Rows and columns represent genes and conditions of the expression matrix respectively. Conditions may belong to different timepoints. Each entry represents the expression level of a gene under a condition. The expression levels for a gene across different experimental conditions are cumulatively called the gene expression profile, and the expression levels for all genes under an experimental condition are cumulatively called the sample expression profile. Figure 1 shows the gene expression matrix.

Fig. 1 **Gene expression matrix**

	Con 1	Con 2	...	...	Con M
Gene 1	$GEx_{1,1}$	$GEx_{1,2}$	...	...	$GEx_{1,M}$
Gene 2	$GEx_{2,1}$	$GEx_{2,2}$	...	...	$GEx_{2,M}$
...	...	...	...	...	...
...	...	...	...	...	...
Gene N	$GEx_{N,1}$	$GEx_{N,2}$	...	...	$GEx_{N,M}$

At the beginning of the process, clustering algorithms have often been used to reduce the complexity of humongous expression data [2]. Clustering techniques have proven to be helpful to understand gene function, gene regulation, cellular processes, and subtypes of cells. The traditional clustering algorithms are not suitable for all applications, especially gene expression data analysis. These clustering algorithms group the genes over all the conditions, whereas cellular processes are active only under a subset of conditions. Also, a single gene may belong to more than one group as a gene may be involved in more than one biological process. Consequently, biclustering algorithms have been offered as another approach to standard clustering techniques to identify local patterns from gene expression data sets. Biclustering refers to the "simultaneous clustering" of both rows and columns of a data matrix. Let G be a set of genes C a set of conditions, and $A(G, C)$ the expression matrix, where $G=\{1,2,...,m\}$ and $C=\{1,2,...,n\}$. The element $GEx_{i,j}$ of $A(G, C)$ represents the expression level of gene 'i' under condition 'j'. The aim of biclustering is to extract the sub-matrix $A(G', C')$ of $A(G, C)$ meeting homogeneity criteria, which is identified by gene subset G' of G and condition subset C' of C.

2. BICLUSTERING METHODS

At present, there are plenty of biclustering techniques available for gene expression data analysis. We make out two main classes of biclustering algorithms: systematic search approaches and stochastic search approaches, also called metaheuristic algorithms. In general, the heuristic search algorithms are used to approximate the problem by finding sub-optimal solutions. Metaheuristics are stochastic optimization it finds a solution in a reasonable time.

Metaheuristics have usually an iterative behavior.

2. Systematic Biclustering Algorithms

2.1.1 Divide and Conquer Approach

Generally, a divide and conquer approach works by recursively breaking down a problem into two or more sub-problems of the same (or related) type, until these become simple enough to be solved directly. The solutions to the sub-problems are then combined to give a solution to the original problem. With this approach, initially a bicluster representing the whole data matrix then it divides into two submatrices to obtain two biclusters. Then reiterate recursively this process until to get a certain number of biclusters verifying a specific set of properties.

The biclustering algorithm called direct clustering is proposed by [3] was one of the first works ever published on biclustering, although it was not applied to gene expression data. The algorithm is based on the use of a divide and conquers approach, in which the input matrix is iteratively partitioned into a set of sub-matrices, until k matrices are obtained, where k is an input parameter for the number of desired biclusters.

The Bimax algorithm is a method for finding subgroups of 1 value in a binary matrix [4]. All values above the threshold will be set to one, all those below to zero. The discretization scheme defines if only down or up-regulated genes (or both) will be considered. Although being very fast, however, its biggest disadvantage is that it may ignore good biclusters by partitioning them before identifying them.

Zhao et al presented a new geometric biclustering algorithm based on the Hough Transform [5]. Based on the linear structures in column-pair spaces and divide them into different patterns using the Additive and Multiplicative Pattern Plot (AMPP). This method reduces the computational complexity considerably and makes it possible to analyze large-scale microarray data.

Yang et al proposed a novel transform technique based on Singular Value Decomposition (SVD) to extract significant biclusters [6]. The whole process includes three steps: property of SVD, the Bidirectional Mixed Clustering algorithm and Lift algorithm. Even though extracting negative correlation gene pairs, however biggest issue is that it may ignore good biclusters by partitioning them and quality of biclusters fully depends on the more number of initial parameter value.

2.1.2 Greedy Iterative Search Approach

This approach builds a solution in a step-by-step way using a given quality measure. Decisions made at each step are based on information at hand without worrying about the effect these decisions may have in the future. Moreover, once a decision is taken, it becomes permanent and is never reconsidered. By applying this approach to the biclustering problem, at each iteration, submatrices of the data matrix are constructed by adding/removing a row/column to/from the current submatrix that maximizes/minimizes a certain function. This process reiterate until no other row/column can be added/removed to/from any submatrix.

Ben-Dor et al defined a bicluster as an Order-Preserving Sub-Matrix (OPSM) [7]. This way, a sub-matrix is said to be order preserving if there is a permutation of its columns under which the sequence of values in every row is strictly increasing. This algorithm can also be used to discover more than one bicluster in the same dataset, even when they are overlapped. However, in this model concerns only the order of values and thus makes the model quite restrictive.

An Iterative Signature Algorithm (ISA) provides a definition of biclusters as transcription modules to be retrieved from the expression data proposed by [8]. It starts with a set of input seeds and the fixed points find corresponding to each seed through iterations. These distinct fixed points are collect in order to decompose the expression data into modules. The structure of this decomposition depends on the choice of thresholds. The first normalization step in ISA may cause increased overlap degree. Because the range of expression values after normalization becomes narrower with increased overlapping, the differences between normal and significant expression values blur and are more difficult to separate.

To address random masking of the values in the data matrix issue and to further accelerate the biclustering process, the authors presented a new model of bicluster to incorporate null values. Yang et al proposed an algorithm named FLexible Overlapped biclustering (FLOC) able to discover a set of k possibly overlapping [9] biclusters simultaneously based on probabilistic moves. Bicluster volume is taken into account within the possible actions, where bigger biclusters are preferred, and the variance is used to reject constant biclusters. The whole process ends when no action that improves the overall quality can be found.

Liu & Wang proposed the Maximum Similarity Bicluster (MSB) algorithm [10]. It starts by constructing a similarity matrix based on a reference gene. Then a process of iteratively remove the row or column in the bicluster with the worst similarity score is perform, until there is one element left in the bicluster. MSB performs well for overlapping biclusters and works well for additive biclusters. But, it works for the special case of approximately squares biclusters. In order to overcome this issue, an extension algorithm named Randomized MSB Extension (RMSBE) algorithm is also presented.

DiMaggio et al presented an approach based on the Optimal RE-Ordering of the rows and columns of a data matrix so as to globally minimize dissimilarity metric [11]. Converse to OPSM, this approach allows for monotonicity violations in the reordering, but penalize their contributions according to a selected objective function. However, the main drawback of this method is that objective function extracts trivial solutions.

Angiulli et al. presented a biclustering algorithm based on a greedy technique enriched with a local search strategy to escape poor local minima named Random Weight Biclustering (RWB) which produces one bicluster at a time [12]. In order to avoid getting trapped into poor local minima, the algorithm executes random moves according to a probability given by the user. Moreover, degree of overlapping rate is controlled for genes and conditions independently by using two different frequency thresholds.

Li et al presented as a QUalitative BIClustering algorithm (QUBIC), in which the input data matrix is first represented as a matrix of integer values, either in a qualitative or semi-qualitative manner [13]. Edge weights are computed in the base of the similarity level between the two corresponding rows. After the graph has been created, biclusters are identified one by one, starting for each bicluster with the heaviest unused edge as a seed. However it delivers approximative solutions without optimality guarantees.

Ayadi et al presented an algorithm BicFinder for extracting biclusters from microarray data which constructs a Directed Acyclic Graph (DAG) to combine a subset of genes under a subset of conditions iteratively [14], by adopting the evaluation function Average Correspondence Similarity Index. BicFinder, do not require fixing a minimum or a maximum number of genes or conditions, enabling a generation of diversified biclusters. However, it places restrictive constraints on the structure of the biclustering solutions.

2.1.3 Biclusters Enumeration Approach

This approach tries to enumerate (explicitly or implicitly) all the solutions for an original problem. The enumeration process is generally represented by a search tree. By applying this approach to the biclustering problem, identify all the possible groups of biclusters in order to keep the best one. This approach has the advantage of being able to obtain the best solutions. Its disadvantage is that it is costly in computing time and in memory space. Tanay et al based their approach on graph theoretic coupled with statistical modeling of the data [15], where SAMBA stands for Statistical Algorithmic Method for Bicluster Analysis. In their work, they framework the input expression data as a bipartite graph whose two parts correspond to conditions and genes, respectively, and edges refer to significant expression changes. This way, discovering the most significant biclusters means finding the heaviest sub-graphs in the model bipartite graph, where the weight of a sub-graph is the sum of the weights of the gene-condition pairs in it.

A MicroCluster algorithm is proposed by [16] as a biclustering method for mining maximal biclusters satisfying certain homogeneity criteria. It follows an enumeration method consisting of three steps. In the first step the multi-graph is created, a second step is applied for mining the maximal clusters from it and final step is optionally executed so as to delete or merge those biclusters according to several overlap conditions. This strategy succeeds in discovering shifting pattern biclusters by using exponential transformations. Even so, there is difficulty to generate scaling pattern.

The BiMine algorithm of Ayadi et al [17] is a method for finding coherent bicluster relies on a new evaluation function called Average Spearman's rho (ASR). It uses a new tree structure, called Bicluster Enumeration Tree (BET), to represent the different biclusters discovered during the enumeration process. Compared to other data structure, BET permits to represent the maximum number of significant biclusters and the links that exist between these biclusters. There is no overlapping control is carried out among the reported solutions.

Ayadi et al proposed a biclustering algorithm, called BiMine+, which is able to detect significant biclusters from gene expression data [18]. The algorithm uses a Modified Bicluster Enumeration Tree (MBET) to represent the identified biclusters, where each node of MBET contains the gene profile shape of a bicluster. The profile shape of a gene is defined as the behavior of this gene, i.e., up, down or no change, over the conditions of the bicluster to which this gene belongs. However, this algorithm is computational time expensive.

A CoBi: Pattern Based Co-Regulated Biclustering is presented by [19] as a biclustering method for grouping both positively and negatively regulated genes from microarray expression data. Regulation pattern and similarity in degree of fluctuation are accounted for while computing similarity between two genes. An advantage of BiClust is that it requires a single pass over the database to generate all biclusters. Nevertheless, the main drawback of this method is that extracts small biclusters for large MSR value.

2.2. Stochastic Biclustering Algorithms

2.2.1 Neighbourhood Search Approach

A neighborhood search, also called local search starts with an initial solution s and then moves iteratively to a neighboring solution. A neighboring solution is generally generated by applying a transformation operator, also called move operator, to the current solution. For instance, the basic hill-climbing strategy replaces the current solution by a neighbouring solution of better quality. By using this approach to the biclustering problem, an initial solution which can be a bicluster or the whole matrix. Then, at each iteration this solution can be improved by adding and/or removing some genes/conditions to minimize/maximize a certain function.

Cheng & Church were the first apply this concept to biclustering to gene expression data. Their goal is to find biclusters with a MSR value lower than a fixed threshold [20]. Hence, they proposed an iterative search procedure which deletes/adds genes/conditions to the biclusters. The single node deletion method iteratively removes the gene or column that has low quality according to MSR. This strategy succeeds in discovering biclusters with coherent values, Since, the algorithm discovers one bicluster at a time, repeated application of the method on a modified matrix is needed for discovering multiple biclusters. This has the drawback that it results in highly overlapping gene sets.

Bryan et al proposed an application of simulated annealing to the biclustering of gene expression data. In this approach, the fitness of each solution is given by its MSR value, and ten times the number of genes successes needed to be achieved before cooling [21]. In their work, they used the same method of Cheng & Church, replacing the original values for random ones, in an attempt to prevent them to be part of any further bicluster.

Liu et al presented their biclustering approach on the use of a PSO together with crowding distance as the nearest neighbour search strategy, which speed up the convergence to the Pareto front and also guarantee diversity of solutions [22]. The author focus on three objectives, the size, homogeneity and row variance of biclusters, are satisfied simultaneously by applying three fitness functions in optimization framework. By using PSO has shown its fast search speed in many complicated optimization and search problems. Even so, there is difficulty to select probable value of inertia weight.

A similar approach to that of Cheng and Church has been followed by Mukhopadhyay et al [23] in order to incorporate a new coherence measure called scaling mean squared residue (SMSR) into a search heuristic. SMSR allows finding biclusters with shifting patterns and also biclusters with scaling patterns, but it does not find biclusters with both kinds of patterns simultaneously.

Ayadi et al [24] presented a Pattern Driven Neighbourhood Search (PDNS) approach for the biclustering problem. PDNS first follows up a preprocessing step to transform the input data matrix to a behavior matrix and a dedicated neighborhood taking into account various patterns information. The algorithm outputs one bicluster at a time. Therefore, in order to obtain several biclusters it must be run several times with different initial solutions. In this work, the authors use the output of two fast well-known algorithms as initial biclusers. Nevertheless, no overlapping control is carried out among the reported solutions.

2.2.2 Evolutionary Computation Approach

The evolutionary computation approach is based on the natural evolutionary process. An evaluation mechanism is established to assess the quality of each individual. Evolution operators eliminate some individuals and produce new individuals from selected individuals. By applying this approach to the biclustering problem, it starts from an initial population of solutions, i.e., biclusters or the whole matrix, then, the quality of each solution of the population can be measured by the fitness function. New solutions are obtained by using recombination and mutation operators. This process ends when a prefixed stop condition is verified.

Bleuler et al were the first in developing an evolutionary biclustering algorithm [25]. They proposed the use of binary strings for the individuals representation, and an initialization of random solutions but uniformly distributed according to their sizes. Bit mutation and uniform crossover are used as reproduction operators, and a fitness function that prioritizes MSR. A diversity maintenance strategy is carried out which decreases the amount of overlapping among bicluster. However, it returns trivial bicluster.

Divina & Aguilar-Ruiz presented as a Sequential Evolutionary BIclustering approach (SEBI) [26]. The term sequential refers the way in which bicluster are discovered, being only one bicluster obtained per each run of the evolutionary algorithm. So as to get many biclusters, a sequential strategy is adopted, invoking several times the evolutionary process. Moreover, a matrix of weights is employed for the control of overlapped elements among the different solutions. This weight matrix is initialized with zero values and is updated every time a bicluster is returned. Even so, it works well for the special case of roughly tiny biclusters.

A Multi-Objective Evolutionary algorithm (MOEA) based on pareto dominance is presented by [27]. Unlike single objective optimization problems, the MOEA tries to optimize two or more conflicting characteristics represented by fitness functions. A local search strategy based on the node insertion and node deletion phases of CC algorithm is applied to all of the individuals at the beginning of every generational loop. In order to maintain diversity in the population, a measure called crowding distance is used. This approach has the advantage of being able to extract a large size of bicluster to a given threshold. However, the main drawback of this method is that converges slowly and consumes much time to find the best solutions.

Biclustering via a Hybrid Evolutionary Algorithm (BiHEA) was proposed by [28] and is very similar to the evolutionary biclustering algorithm of [25]. However, they differ in the crossover operator and integrates gene variance in the fitness function. This method incorporates two mechanisms: the first one avoids loss of good solutions through generations; and the second one is elitism, in which a predefined number of best biclusters are directly passed to next generation without overlap.

Huang et al have proposed a biclustering algorithm based on the use of an Evolutionary Algorithm (EA) together with hierarchical clustering [29]. In this method, the conditions are separated into a number of conditions subsets, also called subspaces. The evolutionary algorithm is then applied to each subspace in parallel, and an expanding and merging phase is finally employed to combine the subspaces results into the output biclusters. So it is called as Condition-Based Evolutionary Biclustering. The parallel computing technology would be of great help to speedup the traditional EA framework. But, its disadvantage is that it is extract small volume of bicluster.

3. CONCLUSIONS

Given the variety of available biclustering algorithms, one of the problems faced by biologists is the selection of the algorithm most appropriate to a given gene expression data set. However, there is no single "best" algorithm which is the "winner" in every aspect. For gene expression data, meta-heuristic approaches would be more appropriate to NP-complete bilustering problem. However, Biological validation of biclusters of microarray data is one of the most important open issues. So far, there are no general guidelines in the literature on how to validate biologically such biclusters.

REFERENCES

[1] D.J. Lockhart, and E.A. Winzeler, "Genomics, gene expression and DNA arrays," Nature, Vol. 405, 2000, pp. 827-836.
[2] D. Jiang, C. Tang and A. Zhang, "Cluster Analysis for Gene Expression Data: A Survey", IEEE Transactions on Knowledge & Data Engineering, Vol. 16, No. 11, 2004, pp. 1370-1386.

[3] J. A. Hartigan, "Direct clustering of a data matrix", Journal of the American Statistical Association, Vol. 67, No. 337, 1972, pp. 123–129.
[4] A. Prelic, S. Bleuler, P. Zimmermann, P. Buhlmann, W. Gruissem, L. Hennig, L. Thiele, and E. Zitzler, "A systematic comparison and evaluation of biclustering methods for gene expression data", Bioinformatics, Vol. 22, No. 9, 2006, 1122–1129, 2006.
[5] H. Zhaoa, A.W. Liewb, X. Xie and H. Yan, "A new geometric biclusteringe algorithm based on the Hough transform for analysis of large-scale microarray data", Journal of Theoritical Biology, Vol. 251, 2008, pp. 264-274.
[6] W.H. Yang, D.Q. Dai, H. and Yan H, "Finding correlated biclusters from gene expression data", IEEE Transactions on Knowledge and Data Engineering, Vol. 23, 2011, pp. 568-584
[7] A. Ben-Dor, B. Chor, R. Karp, and Z. Yakhini, "Discovering local structure in gene expression data: The order-preserving submatrix problem," Journal of Computational Biology, Vol. 10, No. 4, 2003, pp. 373-384.
[8] S. Bergmann, J. Ihmels, and N. Barkai. "Iterative signature algorithm for the analysis of large-scale gene expression data," Physics Review E, Vol. 67, 2003, pp. 1-18.
[9] J. Yang, H. Wang, W. Wang, and P. Yu, "Enhanced biclustering on expression data", In Proceedings of the 3rd IEEE Symposium on BioInformatics and BioEngineering, Washington, DC, USA, 2003, pp. 321-327.
[10] X. Liu, and L. Wang, "Computing the maximum similarity bi-clusters of gene expression data," Bioinformatics, Vol. 23, No. 1, 2007, pp. 50-56.
[11] P. DiMaggio, S. McAllister, C. Floudas, X. Feng, J. Rabinowitz, and H. Rabitz, "Biclustering via optimal reordering of data matrices in systems biology: rigorous methods and comparative studies," Bioinformatis, Vol. 9, No. 1, 2008, pp. 458-467.
[12] F. Angiulli, E. Cesario, and C. Pizzuti, "Random walk biclustering for microarray data", Journal of Information Sciences, Vol. 178, No. 6, 2008, pp. 1479–1497.
[13] G. Li, Q. Ma, H. Tang, A.H. Paterson, and Y. Xu, "Qubic: a qualitative biclustering algorithm for analyses of gene expression data", Nucleic acids research, Vol. 37, No. 15, e. 101.
[14] W. Ayadi, M. Elloumi, and J. K. Hao, "Bicfinder: a biclustering algorithm for microarray data analysis. Knowledge and Information Systems ", Vol. 30, No. 2, 2009, pp 341-358
[15] A. Tanay, R. Sharan, and R. Shamir, "Discovering statistically significant biclusters in gene expression data," Bioinformatics, Vol. 18, 2002, pp. 136-144.
[16] L. Zhao, M. Zaki, "Microcluster: E_cient deterministic biclustering of microarray data", IEEE Intelligent Systems, Vol. 20, No. 6, 2005, pp. 40-49
[17] W. Ayadi, M. Elloumi, and J. K. Hao, "A biclustering algorithm based on a bicluster enumeration tree : Application to DNA microarray data", BioData Mining, Vol. 2, No. 9, 2009.
[18] W. Ayadi, M. Elloumi, and J. K. Hao, "BiMine+: an efficient algorithm for discovering relevant biclusters of DNA microarray data", Knowledge-Based Systems, Vol. 35, 2012, pp. 224-234 .
[19] S. Roy, D.K. Bhattacharyya, and J.K. Kalita, "CoBi: Pattern Based Co-Regulated Biclustering of Gene Expression Data," Pattern Recognition Letter, Vol. 34, No. 14, 2013, pp. 1669-1678.
[20] Y. Cheng and G. M. Church "Biclustering of expression data", In Proceedings of the Eighth International Conference on Intelligent Systems for Molecular Biology, pp. 93–103. AAAI Press, 2000.
[21] K. Bryan, P. Cunningham, and N. Bolshakova, "Application of simulated annealing to the biclustering of gene expression data", IEEE Transactions on Information Technology on Biomedicine, Vol. 10, No. 3, 2006, pp. 519–525.
[22] J. Liu, Z. Li, X. Hu , Y. Chen, "Biclustering of microarray data with mospo based on crowding distance", Bioinformatics, Vol. 10(Suppl 4):S9, 2009.
[23] A. Mukhopadhyay , U. Maulik, S. Bandyopadhyay, "Finding multiple coherent biclusters in microarray data using variable string length multiobjective genetic algorithm", IEEE Transactions on Information Technology in Biomedicine, Vol. 13, No. 6, 2009.
[24] W. Ayadi, M. Elloumi, and J. K. Hao, "Pattern-driven neighborhood search for biclustering of microarray data", Bioinformatics, Vol. 13(Suppl 7):S11, 2011
[25] S. Bleuler, A. Prelic, and E. Zitzler, "An EA framework for biclustering of geneexpression data", In Proceedings of Congress on Evolutionary Computation, pp. 166–173, 2004.
[26] F. Divina, and J.S. Aguilar-Ruiz, "Biclustering of expression data with evolutionary computation," IEEE Transations Knowlede and Data Engineering, Vol. 18, No. 5, 2006, pp. 590-602.
[27] S. Mitra, and H. Banka. "Multi-objective evolutionary biclustering of gene expression data," Pattern Recognition Letter, Vol. 39, No. 12, 2006, pp. 2464-2477.
[28] C. A. Gallo, J. A. Carballido, and I. Ponzoni, "Microarray biclustering: A novel memetic approach based on the pisa platform", In Proceedings of the 7th European Conference on Evolutionary Computation, Machine Learning and Data Mining in Bioinformatics, 2009, pp. 44–55, Berlin, Heidelberg.
[29] Q. Huang, D. Tao, X. Li, and A.W.C. Liew, "Parallelized evolutionary learning for detection of biclusters in gene expression data", IEEE/ACM Transaction Computatonal Biology and Bioinformatics, Vol. 9, No. 1, 2012, pp. 560-570.

YOUR KNOWLEDGE HAS VALUE

- We will publish your bachelor's and master's thesis, essays and papers

- Your own eBook and book - sold worldwide in all relevant shops

- Earn money with each sale

Upload your text at www.GRIN.com and publish for free